Easy Desserts
From Around the World

Easy Cookbooks *for Kids*

Enslow Elementary

Heather Alexander

Library of Congress Cataloging-in-Publication Data

Alexander, Heather, 1967–
  Easy desserts from around the world / Heather Alexander.
    p. cm.— (Easy cookbooks for kids)
  Includes index.
  ISBN 978-0-7660-3765-6
  1. Desserts—Juvenile literature. 2. International cooking—Juvenile literature. 3. Quick and easy cooking—Juvenile literature.
  4. Cookbooks. I. Title.
  TX773.A346 2011   2010039481
  641.8'6–dc22

Paperback ISBN 978-1-59845-270-9

Printed in the United States of America
042012 Lake Book Manufacturing, Inc., Melrose Park, IL

10 9 8 7 6 5 4 3 2

To Our Readers: We have done our best to make sure all Internet Addresses in this book were active and appropriate when we went to press. However, the author and the publisher have no control over and assume no liability for the material available on those Internet sites or on other Web sites they may link to. Any comments or suggestions can be sent by e-mail to comments@enslow.com or to the address on the back cover.

Every effort has been made to locate all copyright holders of material used in this book. If any errors or omissions have occurred, corrections will be made in future editions of this book.

♻ Enslow Publishers, Inc., is committed to printing our books on recycled paper. The paper in every book contains 10% to 30% post-consumer waste (PCW). The cover board on the outside of each book contains 100% PCW. Our goal is to do our part to help young people and the environment too!

Illustration Credits: All photos are from Shutterstock.com, except as noted. ©1999 Artville, LLC, (all maps) pp. 15, 17, 20, 23, 27, 29, 32, 35, 38, 41, 44; ©Clipart.com., pp. 9, 13; iStockphoto.com/©Don Nichols (cookie sheet), p.10; ©2011 Photos.com, a division of Getty Images. All rights reserved., p.14 (pinata), p.33 (jam jars), p.39 (tree); ©Nicole diMella/Enslow Publishers, Inc., p.17 (awkadu); p. 19 (demonstration), p. 32 (kolaczki); iStockphoto.com/©Debbi Smirnoff, p. 18 (coconut); ©Ingram Publishing RF/Photolibrary, p. 21 (rice with mango); ©Bon Appetit/Alamy, p. 23 (strawberries romanoff); Flickr/© Julie Magro, p. 24 (huller);©Nathanael Turpin-Griset/StockFood, p. 29 (bowl of granita); iStockphoto.com/©Greg Nicholas, p. 42 (molasses); United States Department of Agriculture (USDA), p.12

Cover Illustration: Shutterstock.com

Warning: The recipes in this book contain ingredients to which people may be allergic, such as peanuts and milk.

Contents

Introduction: Time to Cook!

Have you ever met someone from another country? Maybe you've seen photos or movies of kids from around the world. They probably seem very different from you. They may speak a different language, wear different clothes, or live in a different kind of house. But there's one thing that all kids share, no matter what part of the world they live in. All kids love dessert!

Food brings the world together. It tells a story about each country. Food can tell you about the climate, the lifestyle, the history, and the crops that are grown in each country. Cooking—and eating—are fun and yummy ways to learn about other cultures.

Each recipe in the book has a section on WHAT YOU NEED— the equipment and ingredients for the recipe—and a section called LET'S COOK! that tells you what to do. Each recipe also has information labeled WHAT'S THIS?, COOKING CLUE, and DID YOU KNOW? These explain new terms and teach you new techniques to make cooking easier.

So tie on an apron and get ready to cook easy desserts from all over the world!

Be Safe!

Whenever you are in the kitchen, there are important safety rules to follow.

1. Always **ask a responsible adult** for permission to cook. Always **have an adult** by your side when you use the oven, the stove, knives, or any appliance.

2. If you have long hair, tie it back. Remove dangling jewelry and tuck in any loose clothing.

3. Always use pot holders or oven mitts when handling anything on the stove or in the oven.

4. Never rush while cutting ingredients. You don't want the knife to slip.

5. Always use a timer if something is cooking in the oven—and stay where you can hear it go off.

6. Never leave the kitchen while the stove is on.

7. ALLERGY ALERT! If you are cooking for someone else, let him or her know what ingredients you are using. Some people have life-threatening allergies to such foods as peanuts and shellfish.

Cooking Tips and Tricks

Whenever you are in the kitchen, there are rules to follow. Even the most experienced chefs follow these rules.

Be Clean:

- Wash your hands before you start. Make sure to also wash your hands after touching raw poultry, meat, or seafood and after cracking eggs. These ingredients may have harmful germs that can make you very sick.

- Wash knives and cutting boards well with soap and water after they've touched these ingredients.

- Rinse all fruits and vegetables under cool water before you use them.

- Make sure your work space is clean before you start.

- Clean up as you cook.

Plan Ahead:

- Read the recipe from beginning to end before you start cooking. Be sure you have all the ingredients and tools you will need before you start.

- If you don't understand something in a recipe, ask an adult for help.

Measuring:

- Measuring dry ingredients: To measure dry ingredients, such as flour and sugar, dip the correct size measuring cup into the ingredient until it is full. Then level off the top of the cup with the flat side of a butter knife. Brown sugar is the only dry ingredient that should be tightly packed into a measuring cup.

- Measuring liquid ingredients: Use a clear glass or plastic measuring cup. Make sure the measuring cup is on a flat surface. Pour the liquid into the cup until it reaches the correct level. Check the measurement at eye level.

- Measuring spoons: Different spoons are different sizes. Be sure you are using a *teaspoon* if the recipe asks for it and not a *tablespoon*.

Mixing:

- Beat: Mix ingredients together *fast* with a wooden spoon, whisk, or an electric mixer.

- Mix: Blend ingredients together with a wooden spoon, an electric mixer, or a whisk.

- Stir: Combine ingredients together with a wooden or metal spoon.

Cooking Basics:

- **Cracking an egg:** Hold the egg in one hand. Crack the eggshell against the side of a bowl. Using both hands, pull the shell apart over the bowl so the yolk and the white drop into the bowl.

- **Greasing a pan:** Spread butter, margarine, shortening, or oil over a baking pan or cookie sheet using a small piece of waxed paper. Or use a spray-on oil. It is often easier (and less messy) to cover a cookie sheet with parchment paper instead. You can find parchment paper in the baking aisle of your market.

- **Greasing and flouring a pan:** Grease a pan as described above. Then pour 1 or 2 tablespoons of flour onto the pan and shake it around so the entire surface is covered. Then hold the pan upside down over the sink or garbage can and tap the back gently so that the extra flour falls out. Tap extra flour out into the sink.

- **Preheat:** Turn the oven on at least 15 minutes before you need to use it.

- **Cool:** After the dessert is baked in the oven, place it on a wire cooling rack until it is no longer hot.

- **Melting butter:** First remove the wrapper. Then put the butter in a microwaveable bowl and microwave on high for 30–45 seconds. You can also melt the butter in a saucepan on the stove using low heat.

Cooking Terms

Cooking has its own vocabulary. Here are some terms you should be familiar with.

chop (verb)—To cut into bite-sized pieces.

cream (verb)—To mix together until creamy.

dice (verb)—To cut into small pieces (smaller than chopped; about ¼ inch).

drizzle (verb)—To pour a small amount of liquid in a stream over a dish.

preheat—To turn on the oven until it reaches the desired temperature before putting in the item to bake.

shred (verb)—To cut into small strips.

simmer (verb)—To cook over low heat just below the boiling point.

Cooking Tools

baking dish

cutting board

muffin pan

juicer

cookie sheet

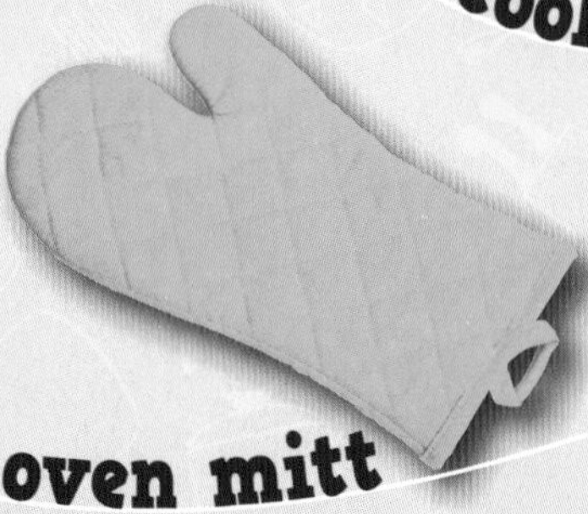

oven mitt

measuring cups

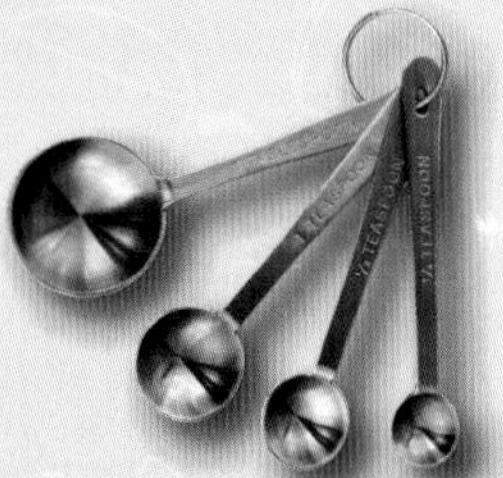

measuring spoons

rubber spatula

paring knife

pastry brush

electric mixer

pie pan

rolling pin

mixing bowls

sauce pan

spatula

whisk

cooling rack

11

Nutrition

The best food is healthy as well as delicious. In planning meals, keep in mind the guidelines of the food pyramid.

MyPyramid
STEPS TO A HEALTHIER YOU
MyPyramid.gov

GRAINS	VEGETABLES	FRUITS	MILK	MEAT & BEANS
Make half your grains whole	**Vary your veggies**	**Focus on fruits**	**Get your calcium-rich foods**	**Go lean with protein**
Eat at least 3 oz. of whole-grain cereals, breads, crackers, rice, or pasta every day	Eat more dark-green veggies like broccoli, spinach, and other dark leafy greens	Eat a variety of fruit	Go low-fat or fat-free when you choose milk, yogurt, and other milk products	Choose low-fat or lean meats and poultry
1 oz. is about 1 slice of bread, about 1 cup of breakfast cereal, or ½ cup of cooked rice, cereal, or pasta	Eat more orange vegetables like carrots and sweet potatoes	Choose fresh, frozen, canned, or dried fruit	If you don't or can't consume milk, choose lactose-free products or other calcium sources such as fortified foods and beverages	Bake it, broil it, or grill it
	Eat more dry beans and peas like pinto beans, kidney beans, and lentils	Go easy on fruit juices		Vary your protein routine — choose more fish, beans, peas, nuts, and seeds

For a 2,000-calorie diet, you need the amounts below from each food group. To find the amounts that are right for you, go to MyPyramid.gov.

Eat 6 oz. every day	Eat 2½ cups every day	Eat 2 cups every day	Get 3 cups every day; for kids aged 2 to 8, it's 2	Eat 5½ oz. every day

Conversions

Recipes list amounts needed. At times you need to know what that amount equals in another measurement. And at other times you may want to cook twice as much (or half as much) as the recipe yields. This chart will help you.

DRY INGREDIENT MEASUREMENTS	
Measure	**Equivalent**
1 tablespoon	3 teaspoons
¼ cup	4 tablespoons
½ cup	8 tablespoons
1 cup	16 tablespoons
2 cups	1 pound
½ stick of butter	¼ cup
1 stick of butter	½ cup
2 sticks of butter	1 cup
LIQUID INGREDIENT MEASUREMENTS	
8 fluid ounces	1 cup
1 pint (16 ounces)	2 cups
1 quart (2 pints)	4 cups
1 gallon (4 quarts)	16 cups

Chapter 1

Celebration Cookies

In Mexico, people hand out small sweet, nutty cookies during celebrations and weddings. Mexican celebration cookies are often wrapped in white, ruffled tissue paper and given to guests.

Another popular part of the celebration is the piñata. A piñata is a brightly colored papier-mâché (*PAY-per muh-SHAY*) container filled with candies and small toys. It is hung from a rope, and children wearing blindfolds swing a stick at the piñata to break it open.

Mexico

Mexico is the northernmost country of Latin America. The Gulf of Mexico and the Caribbean Sea are located on the east, with the Pacific Ocean on its west.

What You Need

Equipment:
Large bowl
Wooden spoon or electric mixer
2 cookie sheets
Plastic or paper bag
Wire cooling rack

Ingredients:
1 cup (2 sticks) unsalted butter, left out of the refrigerator until they are at room temperature
1¾ cups confectioner's sugar
1 teaspoon vanilla extract
2 cups all-purpose flour
¼ teaspoon salt
¾ cup finely chopped pecans

What's This?
Confectioner's sugar is also called powdered sugar.

Cook's Tip
You can use other chopped nuts, such as almonds or walnuts, if you don't have pecans.

Let's Cook!

1. Preheat oven to 350°F (180°C).

2. In a large bowl, beat butter and sugar together until smooth. Use a wooden spoon or an electric mixer (with help from an adult).

3. Add vanilla extract and blend well. Stir in flour and salt; then add pecans. Use your clean hands to blend the dough.

4. Shape the dough into 1-inch balls. Place balls 1 inch apart on ungreased cookie sheets.

5. Bake one sheet at a time for about 20 minutes.

6. While cookies are baking, place confectioner's sugar in a plastic or paper bag.

7. Cool the cookies on a wire rack for 2–4 minutes. While the cookies are still warm, drop three or four into the bag of sugar. Shake the bag to coat the cookies. Return the cookies to the rack to cool completely. Continue until all the cookies are covered by sugar.

Makes 20–24 cookies.

Did You Know?

Many other countries have similar tasting cookies. In the United States, they are called snowballs. In Austria, they are called kipfel (KIP-ful).

Chapter 2

Akwadu
(Banana Coconut Bake)

People in Ghana like to eat akwadu (*ahk-WAH-doo*) after a meal. It is made from bananas and coconut.

Ghana

Ghana is a small country on the west side of Africa. People grow bananas, coconuts, and cola nuts. Cola nuts are used to make many cola drinks.

Bananas

Bananas are the most popular fruit in the world. Over 55 million tons of bananas are eaten each year. Bananas grow on trees in clusters called "hands," and each banana is called a "finger." The word "banana" is Arabic for "finger."

Did You Know?

A banana's flavor is stronger when it is riper. If the banana is ripe, its skin will be yellow with brown spots. Bananas with green peels are not ripe.

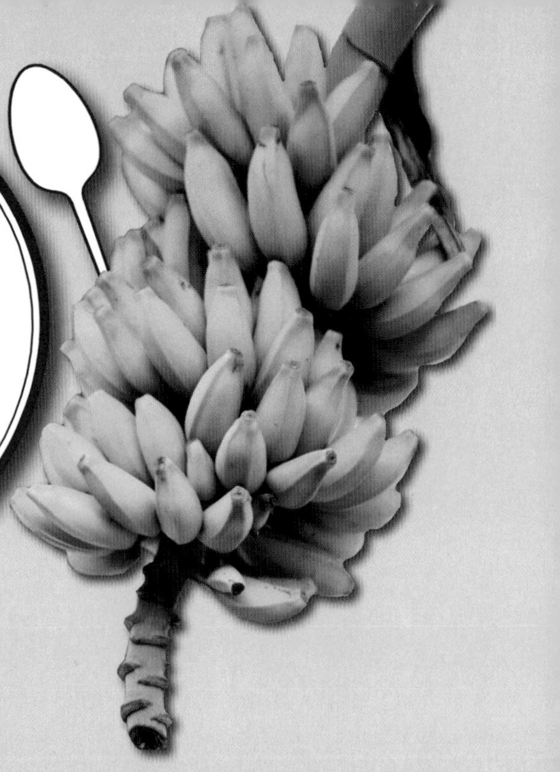

What You Need

Equipment:

9” pie plate or 9” x 9” square baking pan

Small bowl

Spoon

Knife

Ingredients:

5 bananas, peeled

1 tablespoon butter, melted

1 tablespoon lemon juice

⅓ cup orange juice

½ cup brown sugar

1 cup shredded coconut

What's This?

Shredded coconut can be found in the baking aisle of your market.

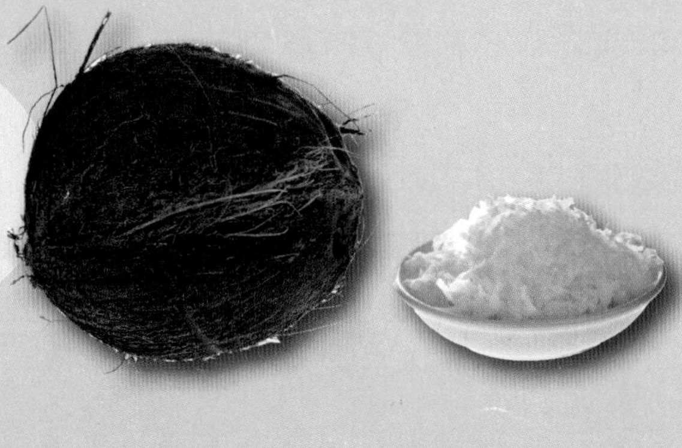

Let's Cook!

1. Place oven rack in the middle of the oven. Preheat oven to 375°F (190°C).

2. Cut the bananas crosswise in half. Then cut each half lengthwise. Place the bananas side by side in the baking pan.

3. Pour melted butter over the bananas.

4. Mix lemon juice and orange juice in a small bowl. Drizzle over the bananas.

5. Sprinkle bananas with brown sugar and coconut.

6. Bake for 8 to 10 minutes or until the coconut is golden brown. Using pot holders or oven mitts, remove the pan from the oven. Spoon bananas and juice into individual bowls. Serve warm.

Makes 4-6 servings.

Cook's Tip

Wait until right before you're ready to cook to peel the bananas. This way the fruit won't turn brown.

Chapter 3

Coconut Sticky Rice With Mango

Rice is a main part of every meal in Thailand. Coconut sticky rice topped with juicy mango is a popular dessert.

Thailand

Thailand is a country in Southeast Asia. It is known for its beautiful white sandy beaches and tropical climate.

Thailand is the largest grower and shipper of rice to other countries. Rice is a grain that is grown in paddies, which are fields flooded with water.

What You Need

Equipment:
2 medium saucepans
(one with a lid)
Large spoon
Knife

Ingredients:
1 cup jasmine rice
14-ounce can coconut milk
5 tablespoons brown sugar
¼ teaspoon salt
1 mango, sliced

What's This?

There are many kinds of rice. Jasmine rice is a sweet rice from Asia. You can use another sweet Asian rice instead.

Did You Know?

Coconut milk is not the juice found inside a coconut. It is the cream that is pressed out of the coconut's white flesh.

Let's Cook!

1. Using a medium saucepan, prepare the rice according to the package directions, except use coconut milk for half of the water. Add 1 tablespoon brown sugar and salt.

2. When there is no liquid left, turn off the heat, but keep the pot on the stove with the cover on.

3. While the rice is cooking, make the sauce. In a medium saucepan, combine the rest of the coconut milk and 4 tablespoons brown sugar. Boil. Stir until it thickens to a syrup.

4. Put a scoop of the sticky rice in each individual bowl. (Ask an adult to slice the mango.) Place several mango slices on top. Then pour the warm coconut sauce over the rice and mango and enjoy.

Makes 4 servings.

Cook's Tip

To make the rice thicker and fluffier, soak it in 1 cup of water for 20 minutes before cooking it.

Chapter 4

Strawberries Romanoff

Strawberries Romanoff is an easy, sweet dessert of juicy, red strawberries topped with whipped cream. The dessert was created in the early 1900s for Russia's ruler, or czar, by his French chef. Romanoff was the last name of the czar's family.

Russia

Russia is a huge country that stretches all the way across the northern part of Asia. Much of the land is covered by forests. Wild berries, including strawberries, grow in the forests.

What You Need

Equipment:

Paring knife and/or strawberry huller

2 medium bowls

Electric mixer

Aluminum foil or plastic wrap

What's This?

A strawberry huller is the utensil used to remove the green leafy stem and the white pulpy inside.

Ingredients:

2 pints ripe strawberries

½ cup orange juice

¼ cup and 1 tablespoon white sugar

1 cup heavy whipping cream

½ teaspoon vanilla extract

Did You Know?

Small and medium-sized strawberries are often sweeter than larger strawberries.

Let's Cook!

1. Wash the berries and pat them dry with paper towels. Hull the berries, then cut them into quarters.

2. Gently combine the berries, orange juice, and ¼ cup sugar in a medium bowl. Cover the bowl with foil or plastic wrap and refrigerate for 2–4 hours.

3. Right before you are ready to serve, beat the whipping cream, vanilla, and 1 tablespoon white sugar in a bowl with an electric mixer until soft peaks form. (Ask an adult to help with this step.)

4. Spoon the berries and some juice into individual bowls. Top with whipped cream and serve.

Makes 8 servings.

Cook's Tip

When hulling a strawberry, use a paring knife to cut a V-shaped wedge down and around the stem.

Chapter 5

ANZAC Biscuits

In Australia, "biscuit" is another name for cookie. These sweet, chewy cookies have been a favorite treat in Australia for almost a hundred years.

ANZAC stands for Australian and New Zealand Army Corps. In 1915, women in Australia and New Zealand created ANZAC biscuits to send to soldiers during World War I. The cookies didn't use eggs or milk, so they wouldn't spoil when they were shipped far away. Plus, they are fast and easy to make!

Did You Know?

ANZAC biscuits are also called soldiers' biscuits.

Australia

Australia is the only country that is a continent. It is an island that lies between the South Pacific Ocean and the Indian Ocean. New Zealand is a smaller island to the west of Australia.

What You Need

Equipment:
2 cookie sheets
Large bowl
Small bowl
Wooden spoon
Wire rack

Ingredients:
1 cup all-purpose flour or whole-wheat flour
1 cup old-fashioned oats
½ cup white sugar
½ cup brown sugar
1 cup shredded coconut
1 teaspoon baking soda
1 stick butter, melted
2 tablespoons honey or golden syrup
2 tablespoons boiling water

Cook's Tip

You can melt the butter in the microwave or in a saucepan on the stove using low heat.

What's This?

Golden syrup is sold in Australia, but it is hard to find elsewhere. You can use honey instead.

Let's Cook!

1. Preheat oven to 350°F (180°C). Grease two cookie sheets or line them with parchment paper.

2. In a large bowl, combine the flour, oats, white sugar, brown sugar, coconut, and baking soda.

3. In a small bowl, mix the melted butter with honey. Add the boiling water. Stir.

4. Pour the liquid mixture over the dry mixture and mix with a wooden spoon until blended.

5. Using clean hands, form 1-inch balls of the dough. Place the balls at least 2 inches apart on the cookie sheets. (These cookies spread a lot while baking.) Press the dough balls slightly with your hands to flatten them.

6. Bake one sheet at a time for 13 minutes or until golden brown. Remove from the oven and let them cool on a wire rack.

Makes 18 cookies.

Chapter 6

Lemon Granita

Lemon granita (*grah-NEE-tah*) is a sweet and tart dessert from Italy. The shaved ice tastes like a lemonade slushie. This frosty treat is perfect for a hot summer day.

Italy

Italy is in the southern part of Europe. It is a peninsula, meaning the land is surrounded by water on three sides.

This dessert comes from southern Italy, an area that has many lemon groves. Lemons are a citrus fruit that has lots of vitamin C.

What You Need

Equipment:
Knife
Juicer
Saucepan
Wooden spoon
8" x 8" metal baking pan
Fork

Ingredients:
8 lemons
3 cups water
2 cups white sugar

What's This?
Juicers make squeezing lemons, limes, and oranges much easier.

Let's Cook!

1. Cut the lemons in half. Squeeze out all the juice using a juicer. Make sure there are no pits in the juice. You should have 1½ cups fresh lemon juice.

2. Pour the water and sugar into a saucepan. Over low heat, stir until the sugar dissolves or until you can no longer see the sugar crystals.

Cook's Tip

You can get more juice out of a lemon if you roll it on the countertop before squeezing it.

3. Remove from the heat and add in the lemon juice. Stir.

4. Pour the mixture into the pan. Carefully place the pan flat in the freezer.

5. Freeze for 1 hour. Take the pan out of the freezer and scrape the lemon ice with a fork to break up the chunks. Return the pan to the freezer. Scrape the ice once an hour for 6 hours. The ice should be in crystals or flakes. It should not be smooth.

6. Spoon lemon granita into dessert bowls. You can serve with a mint leaf or slice of lemon on top.

Makes 4-5 servings.

Did You Know?

The lemon granita serves better if you first chill the dessert bowls in the freezer.

Chapter 7

Kolaczki Cookies

Kolaczki (*koh-LAHCH-kee*) are flaky cookies dusted with powdered sugar. They have a sweet jelly surprise inside. These cookies from Poland are sometimes called "Polish foldovers."

Poland

Poland is a large country in the center of Europe. It is covered by lots of farmland.

Kolaczki are traditional Christmas cookies in Poland. On Christmas Eve, the Polish people eat a huge dinner, followed by many desserts. It is a custom not to begin eating on Christmas Eve until the first star is spotted in the night sky.

What You Need

Equipment:
Medium mixing bowl
Electric mixer
Plastic wrap
Rolling pin
Knife
Pastry brush
2 cookie sheets

Ingredients:
1 cup (2 sticks) butter, left out of the refrigerator until they are at room temperature

3 ounces (small package) cream cheese, left out of the refrigerator until it becomes soft (about 70–75°F)

1¾ cups all-purpose flour

Confectioner's sugar

½ cup jam

1 egg white

What's This?

A pastry brush looks like a paintbrush, except it's only used on food.

Cook's Tip

Be adventurous! Try any flavor jam you have at home— strawberry, raspberry, apricot, blueberry, lemon— whatever you like.

Let's Cook!

1. With an adult's help, beat the butter and cream cheese with an electric mixer at low speed until fluffy. Slowly mix in the flour.

2. With clean hands, form the dough into a ball and cover with plastic wrap. Refrigerate the dough for 1 hour.

3. Preheat oven to 350°F (180°C).

4. Dust a clean, flat surface with confectioner's sugar. Divide the dough into several chunks. Using a rolling pin, roll out the dough to ¼-inch thickness. Make sure the dough is thin.

5. Cut the dough into squares 2 inches on each side. Place the squares 2 inches apart on parchment-lined baking pans. Place ½ teaspoon of jam in the center of each square.

6. With a pastry brush, brush the egg white onto two opposite corners of the dough. Pinch the two corners tightly together in the center over the filling. (The egg white will act as "glue" to help keep the corners together.)

7. Bake for 15 minutes. When the corners of the cookies are brown, remove the cookie sheet with pot holders or oven mitts. Cool the cookies and then dust them with confectioner's sugar.

Did You Know?

You should eat or freeze these cookies within a day or two because they don't store well.

Makes 24 cookies.

Chapter 8

Baklava

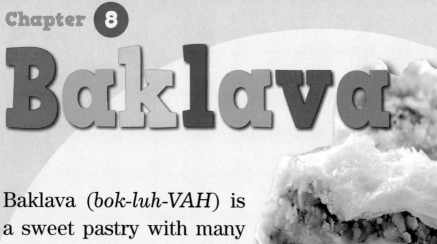

Baklava (*bok-luh-VAH*) is a sweet pastry with many flaky layers of crust filled with nuts, honey, and sugar. Baklava looks like it is difficult to make, but it's not. The key is having everything ready before you start.

Baklava is known as a Greek dessert, but people in countries throughout the Mediterranean, such as Turkey, Bulgaria, Syria, and Lebanon, also enjoy this delicious treat. Some countries make it with crushed pistachios instead of walnuts.

Greece

Greece is located on the southernmost tip of Europe. It is the birthplace of one of the oldest civilizations and home of the first Olympic Games.

What You Need

Equipment:

Medium mixing bowl

Small bowl for melted butter

Pastry brush

9" x 13" baking pan

Damp towel

Medium saucepan

Spoon

Ingredients:

For pastry:

3 cups ground walnuts

1 teaspoon cinnamon

¼ teaspoon nutmeg

½ cup sugar

1½ cups butter, melted

1-pound box phyllo pastry dough

What's This?

Phyllo (FEE-low) means "leaf" in Greek. The dough is leaf thin. You can buy phyllo dough in the frozen food section of the market.

For syrup:

1½ cups water

1½ cups sugar

½ cup honey

¼ teaspoon cinnamon

Let's Cook!

1. Preheat the oven to 300°F (149°C).
2. In a medium bowl, combine the walnuts, cinnamon, nutmeg, and sugar.
3. Using a pastry brush, brush the bottom of a 9" x 13" pan with melted butter.
4. Take out 6 sheets of phyllo pastry. Gently brush each sheet with butter. Stack one sheet on top of the other in the pan.
5. Sprinkle 1 cup of the nut mixture on the top sheet. Stack five more sheets of buttered phyllo on top. Then sprinkle another cup of the nut mixture. Then add five sheets of buttered phyllo and another cup of nut mixture. Repeat this until the nut mixture is finished.
6. Brush the final 6 sheets of phyllo with butter and stack on top. With an adult's help, use a sharp knife to cut the baklava into a diamond pattern.
7. Bake for 1 hour or until the baklava is golden brown.
8. While the baklava is in the oven, place all the syrup ingredients into a medium saucepan. Bring to a boil. Reduce the heat and simmer for 15 minutes. Let the syrup cool.
9. Using oven mitts or pot holders, remove the baklava from the oven. Pour the syrup evenly over the baklava and let it sit for at least 30 minutes before serving. Baklava is often best when made a day ahead.

Makes 24 pieces.

Cook's Tip

Phyllo dough dries out easily. Use one sheet at a time, and cover the dough you are not using with a damp cloth so it stays moist.

Chapter 9

Maple Butter Tarts

Maple butter tarts are a treat from Canada. The small pastries are filled with a sweet, buttery, maple mixture. Tarts look like miniature pies and are meant to be picked up with your hands and eaten in a few bites.

Canada

Canada is a huge country in North America, bordering the United States. Much of Canada is covered by forests. Sugar maple trees, which give maple syrup, grow all over the country. Canada produces the most maple syrup in the world. Its flag even has a huge sugar maple leaf on it.

Did You Know?

Maple syrup comes from the sap of maple trees. Sap is a sweet, sticky liquid inside the tree.

What You Need

Equipment:

Cookie sheet or muffin pan and round cookie cutter

Large mixing bowl

Electric mixer

Spoon

Ingredients:

12 premade tart shells or 2 premade pie crusts(removed from the refrigerator until the shells reach room temperature)

¼ cup (½ stick) unsalted butter at room temperature

½ cup light brown sugar, packed

2 eggs

1 teaspoon vanilla extract

1 cup maple syrup

½ cup diced walnuts

Cook's Tip

Once a bottle of maple syrup is opened, it should be refrigerated.

What's This?

You can find packaged diced walnuts in the baking aisle of the market.

Let's Cook!

1. Preheat oven to 375°F (190°C).

2. Arrange premade tart shells on a cookie sheet. If you are using premade pie crusts, first grease the muffin tin or spray with nonstick spray. Unroll the two pie crusts on a floured surface. Cut six circles with the cookie cutter from each crust. Press the 12 circles of crust into the bottom of the muffin tins and about halfway up the sides.

3. In a large bowl, beat butter and sugar with an electric mixer until creamy. (Get help from an adult when using the mixer.) Blend in eggs, vanilla extract, and syrup.

4. Sprinkle some diced walnuts on the bottom of each tart shell. Then pour in the filling.

5. Bake the tarts for 20 minutes. Remove them from oven using pot holders or oven mitts. Cool on a wire rack. Remove tarts from muffin tin and enjoy.

Makes 12 tarts.

Chapter 10

Lebkuchen
(German Gingerbread Cake)

Gingerbread, called lebkuchen (*LEB-koo-ken*) in Germany, is a moist, spicy cake that is often served during Christmastime. The rich cake is made with many spices, including ginger, cinnamon, and cloves.

Germany

Germany is a large country in central Europe. The city of Nuremberg in Germany is known as the Gingerbread Capital of the World. In the 1600s, the bakers in Nuremberg created amazing houses and scenes out of gingerbread.

What You Need

Equipment:
8" x 8" baking pan
Whisk
Medium mixing bowl
Large mixing bowl
Electric mixer

Ingredients:
2½ cups all-purpose flour
2 teaspoons baking soda
2 teaspoons powdered ginger
1 teaspoon cinnamon
½ teaspoon ground cloves
¼ teaspoon nutmeg
½ cup (1 stick) unsalted butter, room temperature
½ cup light brown sugar, packed
1 cup dark molasses
1 cup boiling water
2 eggs, beaten

What's This?

Molasses is a thick, brown, honeylike syrup made from sugar.

Let's Cook!

1. Preheat oven to 350°F (180°C).

2. Grease and flour an 8" x 8" baking pan.

3. Whisk together flour, baking soda, and spices in a medium bowl.

4. In a large bowl, beat butter and sugar with an electric mixer until fluffy. Add molasses and beat well. Slowly add boiling water and beat. (Get an adult's help for this step.)

5. Add flour mixture and beat until batter is creamy. Add eggs and beat.

6. Pour batter in prepared pan and bake on middle rack in oven for 45–50 minutes.

7. Remove with oven mitts or pot holders and let cool. Gingerbread can be served warm or cold. Try it with some whipped cream on top!

Makes one cake.

Cook's Tip

Poke a clean toothpick into a cake to test if it is done. If the toothpick comes out dry, the cake is ready to take out of the oven.

Chapter 11

Alfajores

Alfajores (*AL-fa-HO-rays*) are sandwich cookies made with two round buttery cookies and a gooey, delicious filling of "dulce de leche" (*DOOL-say day LAY-chay*). Dulce de leche is a milky, caramel-like spread.

Alfajores are enjoyed throughout South America, especially in Argentina. Dulce de leche is as popular in Argentina as peanut butter is in the United States. It is often called "the national sweet."

Argentina

Argentina is the second largest country in South America in area. Argentina has a long, tapered shape and occupies most of the southern part of South America.

What You Need

Equipment:
Cookie sheets
Parchment paper
Medium bowl
Large bowl
Electric mixer
Small spoon
Knife

Ingredients:
2 cups all-purpose flour
¼ teaspoon salt
½ teaspoon baking powder
¾ cup (1½ sticks) unsalted butter, left out of the refrigerator until it reaches room temperature
1 cup white sugar
1 egg
1¼ teaspoons vanilla extract
Confectioner's sugar
Dulce de leche

What's This?

Dulce de leche is sweetened condensed milk that has been boiled for several hours. It means "milk candy" in Spanish. Dulce de leche can be found in most Latin American grocery stores.

Let's Cook!

1. Preheat oven to 350°F (180°C). Line two cookie sheets with parchment paper or grease generously.

2. In a medium bowl, stir flour, salt and baking powder together.

3. In a large bowl, cream butter and sugar until fluffy with an electric mixer (under adult supervision). Beat in egg and vanilla extract. Slowly add flour mixture, a bit at a time.

4. With clean hands, form dough into ¾-inch balls and place on cookie sheet about 1 inch apart. Using the back of a spoon, flatten each dough ball.

5. Bake for 11–12 minutes. Using oven mitts or pot holders, remove the cookies from the oven and cool completely on wire racks before adding filling.

6. Spread 2 teaspoons of dulce de leche filling on one cookie with a knife. Gently press another cookie on top, forming a sandwich. Sprinkle cookies with confectioner's sugar.

Makes 18 cookies.

Cook's Tip

Traditional alfajores are shaped by circular cookie cutters. Because you are not using cookie cutters, try to make your balls of dough as round as possible.

Further Reading

Books

D'Amico, Joan, and Karen Eich Drummond. *The Coming to America Cookbook: Delicious Recipes and Fascinating Stories From America's Many Cultures.* Hoboken, N.J.: John Wiley & Sons, Inc., 2005.

De Mariaffi, Elisabeth. *Eat It Up! Lip-Smacking Recipes for Kids.* Toronto, Canada: Owlkids, 2009.

Dodge, Abigail Johnson. *Around the World Cookbook.* New York: DK Publishing, 2008.

Lagasse, Emeril. *Emeril's There's a Chef in My World!: Recipes That Take You Places.* New York: HarperCollins Publishers, 2006.

Wagner, Lisa. *Cool Sweets & Treats to Eat: Easy Recipes for Kids to Cook.* Edina, Minn.: ABDO Publishing Co., 2007.

Internet Addresses

Cookalotamus Kids

<http://www.cookalotamus.com/kids.html>

PBS Kids: Café Zoom

<http://pbskids.org/zoom/activities/cafe/>

Spatulatta.com

<http://www.spatulatta.com/>

Index